The
Robins
In Your
Backyard

Acknowledgements

My very special thanks to the following people for their editorial and curatorial reviews:
Sally Conyne: Director, Ornithological Education, Academy of Natural Sciences, Philadelphia, PA
Lynne Frink: President, Tri-State Bird Rescue & Research, Inc., Newark, DE
Lynda Graham-Barber: writer and friend
Gene K. Hess: Collections Manager, Delaware Museum of Natural History, Wilmington, DE
Sallie Welte, VMD: Associate Director, Tri-State Bird Rescue & Research, Inc., Newark, DE

for Jennifer, Kristin and James

The Robins In Your Backyard

Summary: Describes a year in the life of a pair of robins as they build a nest, lay eggs and care for their young.

Library of Congress Catalog Card Number: 98-96032

ISBN 0-9662761-0-8 Cloth
(originally published by Cucumber Island Storytellers, ISBN 1-1887813-21-7)

ISBN 0-9662761-1-6 Paper

Published in the United States by Birdsong Books

Printed in Korea

The
Robins
In Your
Backyard

Nancy Carol Willis

Birdsong Books
Middletown, Delaware

On a frosty March morning,
patches of crunchy snow
lie on brown grass.

"*Cheerily, cheer-up, cheerily,*"
sings the robin redbreast to
herald springtime's arrival.

Every spring, robins fly north from their southern home to nest in the land where they were born.

Some robins migrate over 1,000 miles in two weeks. To guide them, the birds use rivers, mountains and coastlines, like road maps.

When they arrive, the robins are tired and hungry. Scratch, poke, plunge! The robin gulps a hatching insect.

Before long the male robin claims a territory. "*Cheerily*, this yard is mine," he sings. His song attracts several females, but only one will choose him as her mate. Together they begin to make a nest.

The female selects the fork of an evergreen branch. It's well-hidden where people and animals will not disturb it. She weaves twigs softened by morning dew. Her mate brings straw and bits of string.

Next, she packs the inside of the nest with wet mud. She presses her body against the sides to form a cup. Finally, she lines the nest with fine, soft grasses.

Several days have passed, and now there are three shiny, blue eggs in the nest. The eggs stay warm under mother robin's breast feathers. From time to time, she rolls each egg to keep it warm all over so that the baby inside can grow.

If you could look inside the egg, you'd see a tiny embryo and a yellow yolk surrounded by watery liquid. The yolk provides food for the embryo as it grows into a bird.

A hungry squirrel has climbed too close to the nest.

"*Tuk, tuk, tuk, teeeek*!" cries the male robin.
Neighboring robins snap their beaks and dive-bomb
the intruder.

"*Cheech, chich, chich*!" cries the
tormented squirrel. He scampers
down the tree to look for food
somewhere else. Squirrels,
snakes, raccoons, blue jays and
crows like to eat robin eggs.

13

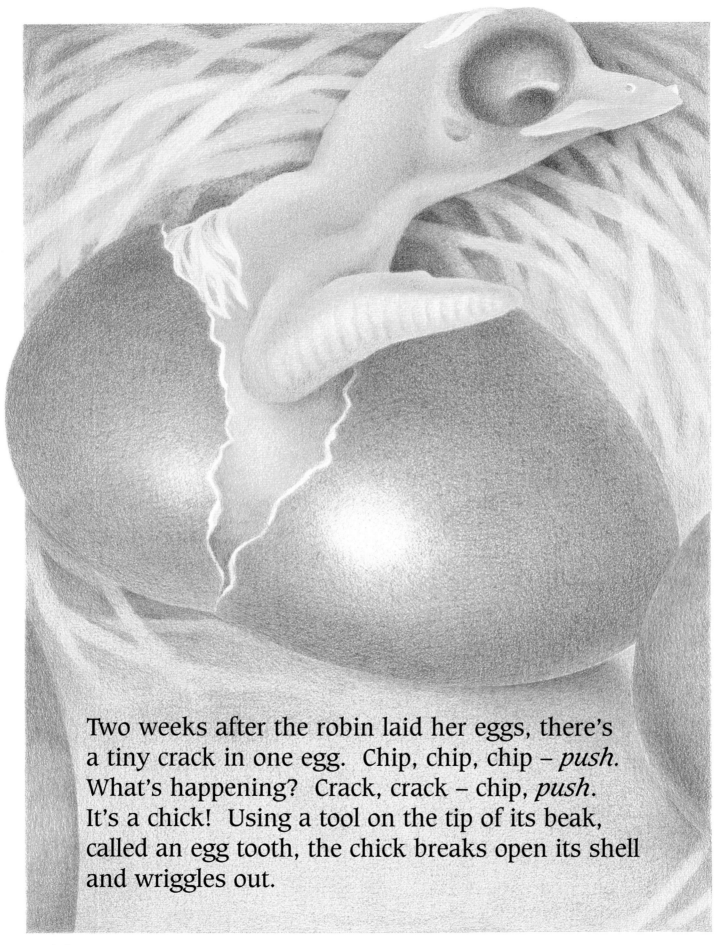

Two weeks after the robin laid her eggs, there's
a tiny crack in one egg. Chip, chip, chip – *push*.
What's happening? Crack, crack – chip, *push*.
It's a chick! Using a tool on the tip of its beak,
called an egg tooth, the chick breaks open its shell
and wriggles out.

The baby robins are weak and helpless. Their eyes are closed and only a few downy feathers cover their pink skin. If you hold a nickel, that's how much a newly hatched robin weighs.

In six days, the robins' eyes open and their feathers start to grow.

Nestling robins grow really fast. If you grew at the same rate, you would weigh 90 pounds by the time you were ten days old!

At night, the babies snuggle under mother robin's wings and body feathers. Her mate sleeps in a nearby tree, along with other neighborhood male robins.

Feeding baby robins keeps both parents busy.
Every ten minutes from sunrise to sunset, they feed
earthworms, insects and juicy berries to their hungry
babies. The young robins stretch their necks,
clamoring for food. Each can eat fourteen feet of
earthworms in one day.

19

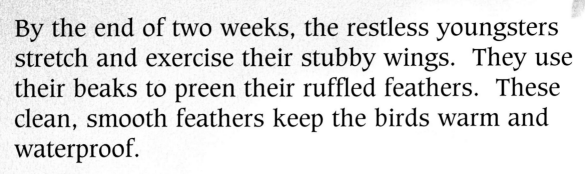

By the end of two weeks, the restless youngsters stretch and exercise their stubby wings. They use their beaks to preen their ruffled feathers. These clean, smooth feathers keep the birds warm and waterproof.

The time to leave the nest has arrived. Hop, flutter, plop!

Learning to fly can be dangerous. Bad weather and predators like cats are the young robins' greatest enemies. Father robin scurries about for two more weeks while he feeds and protects his rowdy brood.

Nature also protects the fledglings. See how their speckled breast feathers camouflage them among light-dappled blades of grass?

The robin fledglings are now fully grown. They can find their own food and no longer mistake twigs for tasty caterpillars.

Unlike humans, the robin's eyes are on the sides of its head. The robin cocks its head when hunting, then – snatch – the prey is gone!

25

The young robins
stay in their territory
throughout the summer.

Meanwhile, their parents
build a new nest and
raise another family.

It's now September. The young robins' speckled feathers are replaced by charcoal gray and brick-red feathers like those of their parents. The shorter, cooler days signal that it's time for the robins to begin their long journey south.

How we miss their morning melody!

"Cheerily, cheer-up, cheerily."

Perhaps you'll be the first to
hear their happy song when
the robins return next spring.

How to Help a Baby Songbird

Let Parents Do Their Job

Do everything you can to leave a young bird with its parents. Return naked nestlings to the nest. A parent bird will not reject the nestling just because it was handled by a human.

A fledgling bird is like a child. It leaves the nest, curious about the world around it, but still dependent on its parents for survival. The parents teach it to find food, recognize danger and adapt to its surroundings. With three or four young birds to watch, a parent may briefly lose track of one. If you find a newly feathered bird on the lawn, watch from a window to see if adult birds are nearby and if they return to feed the baby.

Baby Birds Need Professional Care

If you find an injured or orphaned baby bird, you'll need to take it to a wildlife rehabilitator. Just as veterinarians are trained to care for dogs and cats when they are sick, wildlife rehabilitators are trained to care for wild animals.

- Place the bird on tissues in a small box with air holes if it is a nestling.

- Place the bird on paper towels in a box with air holes if it is a fledgling.

- Keep the bird warm, but out of direct sunlight. (Do not place the bird in the oven or on the stove.)

- Keep the bird away from people and pets.

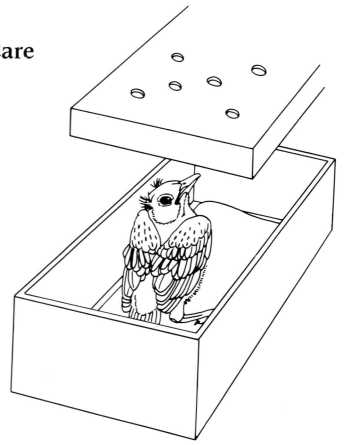

Emergency Feeding

Very young birds need to be fed every ten minutes during daylight hours. If you can't bring the bird to a licensed rehabilitator immediately, feed it this *temporary* diet: Mix a finely mashed hard-cooked egg yolk with 1/3 cup chopped beef canned dog food. Feed the bird tiny pieces of this mixture from a child's watercolor brush or the blunt end of a flat toothpick.

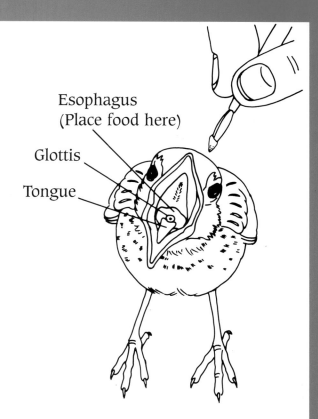

Esophagus
(Place food here)

Glottis

Tongue

- Keep a firm grip on the brush or toothpick and place the food far back in the gaping mouth, above the tongue.
- Wait for the bird to swallow before giving it more food.
- Do not give milk or bread to baby birds. (They can't digest it.)
- Never squirt liquids into a bird's mouth (It can cause pneumonia.)

Cats Cause Many Bird Injuries

Over 20% of the birds brought to wildlife rehabilitators are injured by cats. Cat bites damage bones, organs, skin and feathers. They also cause serious infection that requires immediate professional treatment. If your cat catches a bird, take the following action:

- Poke some holes in a large brown paper bag.

- Place the bird in the bag and fold over the top to prevent escape.

- Take the bird immediately to your nearest licensed rehabilitator.

Who To Contact For Help

Migratory birds are protected by federal law. They are difficult to care for and may be kept only by licensed rehabilitators. If you can't return a bird to the wild, please contact your state or provincial wildlife agency for the name of your local wildlife rehabilitation facility. Also, the National Wildlife Rehabilitators Association (NWRA) can help you find a professional rehabilitator. Contact the NWRA at 14 North 7th Avenue, St. Cloud, MN 56303, USA, (612) 259-4086. Finally, you may contact your local chapter of the Audubon Society, zoo or veterinarian.

Reprinted with permission by Tri-State Bird Rescue & Research, Inc., copyright, 1993

Glossary

Page 4	**Herald**	*v.*	To proclaim or announce important news.
Page 6	**Migrate**	*v.*	To change location seasonally.
Page 7	**Territory**	*n.*	An area of land, often including a nest site, that is defended by an animal.
Page 11	**Embryo**	*n.*	An animal in its earliest stages of growth, before birth or hatching.
Page 12	**Intruder**	*n.*	An unwanted visitor.
Page 13	**Torment**	*v.*	To cause distress or suffering
Page 14	**Egg tooth**	*n.*	A sharp, pointy bump on the tip of the beak used to break through the eggshell.
Page 15	**Downy**	*adj.*	Soft and fluffy.
Page 16	**Nestling**	*n.*	A bird too young to leave the nest.
Page 18	**Clamor**	*n.*	A loud, continuous noise.
Page 20	**Preen**	*v.*	To smooth or clean feathers with the beak.
Page 22	**Brood**	*n.*	The young of a bird hatched at one time.
		v.	1. To sit on an egg in order for it to hatch; 2. To cover young with the wings in order to protect them from heat or rain.
Page 22	**Predator**	*n.*	One that preys, destroys or devours.
Page 22	**Rowdy**	*adj.*	Loud and noisy.
Page 23	**Camouflage**	*n.*	Appearance or behavior designed to conceal or hide.
Page 23	**Dappled**	*adj.*	Marked with spots or patches different from the background.
Page 23	**Fledgling**	*n.*	A young bird reared until ready for flight or independent activity.
Page 23	**Speckled**	*adj.*	Marked with spots.
Page 24	**Prey**	*n.*	An animal taken for food by a predator.
Page 31	**Esophagus**	*n.*	Passageway from the mouth to the stomach.
Page 31	**Glottis**	*n.*	Opening to the vocal cords.

Time Line

Robins arrive at northern breeding grounds	Nest building (4-6 days) Egg laying (1 per day up to 4) Incubation (12-13 days)				Robins build second nest and raise second brood of chicks		Robins roost and feed		
MAR	**APR**	**MAY**	**JUN**	**JUL**	**AUG**	**SEP**	**OCT**		
	Males claim territories and court females	Hatching (All in 1 day) Nestling (12-14 days) Fledgling (10 -19 days)			Robins molt (Replace feathers)		Robins migrate southward		